JEFF
GORDON

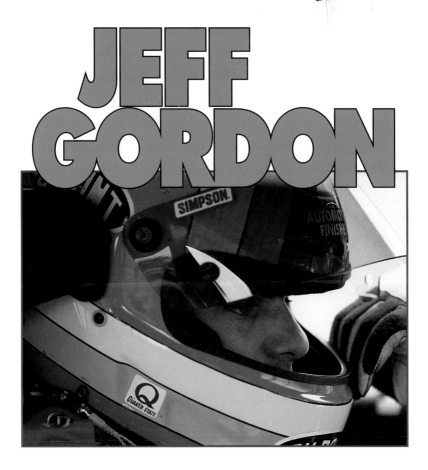

JEFF GORDON

Racing's Superstar

Jeff Savage

LERNER
SPORTS
A DIVISION OF LERNER PUBLISHING GROUP

This book is available in two editions:
Library binding by Lerner Publications Company
Soft cover by First Avenue Editions
Divisions of Lerner Publishing Group
241 First Avenue North
Minneapolis, Minnesota 55401 U.S.A.

Website address: www.lernerbooks.com

Library of Congress Cataloging-in-Publication Data

Savage, Jeff, 1961–
    Jeff Gordon: racing's superstar / Jeff Savage.
      p. cm.
    Includes bibliographical references and index.
    Summary: Biography of the young stock car driver who has won three NASCAR championships and more than forty races in four years.
    ISBN 0–8225–3679–X (lib. bdg. : alk. paper)
    ISBN 0–8225–9859–0 (pbk. : alk. paper)
    1. Gordon, Jeff, 1971—Juvenile literature. 2. Automobile racing drivers—United States—Biography—Juvenile literature. [1. Gordon, Jeff, 1971– 2. Automobile racing drivers] I. Title.
GV1032.G67 S28 2000
796.72'092—dc21   99–050511

Manufactured in the United States of America
1 2 3 4 5 6 – JR – 05 04 03 02 01 00

Contents

Driving His Heart Out

Jeff Gordon was driving hard, on and off the throttle, muscling his rainbow-colored race car through traffic at Daytona International Speedway. Jeff's number 24 car was running third, right on the tail of Rusty Wallace and Dale Jarrett, midway through the 1999 Daytona 500. Jeff came off Turn 2 and went fast with the pack down the **backstretch** at 190 miles an hour. His car rumbled like a mini-earthquake. The five-point safety harness strapped around his body kept him pinned in his seat. The smell of exhaust fumes and burning rubber filled the car's cockpit where the temperature hit a blistering 130 degrees.

Jeff squeezed the steering wheel tighter and made

a move on the high side of Turn 4 to try to pass Jarrett. But nobody went with him to help him draft, and the force of air pushed Jeff back behind two cars into fifth place. Drafting is a technique that a driver can use to reduce the wind resistance on a car. The driver must pull in behind a competitor in order to follow in that car's wind stream. But in this race, drivers did not draft with Jeff. They were afraid to give him any help, even if it helped them too. With any help, Jeff would surely win the race. The other drivers would have to battle for second place. Jeff pressed the button to radio his crew chief, Ray Evernham, in the pit.

"We've got no friends out here," he shouted over the roar of engines around him.

"Yeah," his crew chief replied, "but you knew that."

The other racers in the 42-car field knew that Jeff Gordon is the best race car driver in the world. No racer has ever been so successful at such a young age. Jeff's three NASCAR championships and 47 wins in four years make him the best driver in a generation. His three straight seasons of 10-plus victories are unmatched in the modern era. And his 13 victories in 1998, when he was 26 years old, tied a record set by Richard Petty, "The King" of NASCAR.

Jeff leads the pack at the 1999 Daytona 500.

NASCAR stands for National Association for Stock Car Auto Racing. Stock cars are souped-up versions of real Fords, Chevys, and other cars that regular people drive on the street. Stock cars look like regular street cars except for the decals plastered on them. The difference is under the hood. Cars on the street have about 200-**horsepower** engines. Stock car engines have more than 700 horsepower.

NASCAR stages 33 races each year at tracks across the United States. Drivers collect points for leading a lap, leading the most laps, and for the place they finish. The driver with the most points at the end of the season wins NASCAR's championship.

Back in the blast-furnace cockpit at Daytona, Jeff flipped a switch beside his seat that pumped outside air through tubing into his helmet while blowing exhaust out of the car. But he didn't run the blower system for long because it sucked up power. Every drop of gasoline was precious.

Jeff was running in fourth place on lap 135 and looking for an opening. Then, a car skidded and smacked into a second car, which set off a chain reaction of crunches and flying metal. Jeff avoided the crash by driving low on the **apron.** He saw in his rearview mirror that nearly a dozen cars had turned the track into a demolition derby. The yellow caution flag came out, signaling that cars could not pass one another until the wreckage was cleared off the track.

Jeff pulled in for a **pit stop.** A crew of seven jumped over the pit wall and surrounded Jeff's car with power tools and fresh tires. A crew member handed Jeff cold water and cool towels while the crew frantically filled his gas tank and replaced all four tires in less than 20 seconds. Jeff popped the clutch and zoomed back onto the track.

To maintain his edge, Jeff must make quick pit stops.

The green flag came out on lap 143, meaning the race was back on. Jeff was in fifth place. "The key in a race," Jeff says, "is to tell yourself to be calm, be calm, be calm. And just have a lot of patience to let the race unfold."

Jeff has nerves of steel. His relentless pursuit of checkered flags makes him a modern-day daredevil. He has a special feel for driving, a sort of sixth sense. As one crew chief explains it, "Jeff has a good car and a good crew, which is a big part of his success. But he also has something extra, like Michael Jordan and Mickey Mantle had. He has a different sense of time than you and I. He can slow the race down in his mind, see things coming around, and react before the next guy."

The Daytona 500 is the world's most important stock car race. NASCAR races began half a century earlier in the Florida beach town of Daytona. Stock car racing itself began in the southern part of the United States. During Prohibition, selling or drinking alcohol was illegal. Despite the law, some people made alcohol and had to try to outrun sheriffs on back country dirt roads. These drivers modified their cars to go faster and turn more sharply. Some of these modifications were then adapted for racing cars. NASCAR is still very popular in the South, but Jeff is a big reason why stock car racing's popularity has spread.

Jeff stands 5 feet, 7 inches tall and is handsome with a sparkle in his dark eyes. His wholesome appearance prompts companies to give him millions of dollars to help sell their products. Jeff represents makers of cereal, soda, sunglasses, ice cream, potato chips, and toothpaste. He says he could sell far more products, but he chooses not to. He doesn't want his picture "to be in every single aisle at the supermarket."

Soft-spoken and religious, Jeff has a genuine interest in others. But at the racetrack, he is a fierce competitor and he is easily one of the most popular racers. Mobs of fans ask him to sign his autograph on posters, hats, shirts, even their arms so they can later have it tattooed on.

Jeff gives back to his fans by signing autographs.

Not everyone in the stands likes to see Jeff win, but he doesn't let that affect his racing.

Many of the 110,000 fans in the stands and the 50,000 in the infield at the Daytona track were rooting for Jeff. There are also thousands of fans at every race that don't like him. They complain that he wins too much and he's too rich. They call him a "pretty boy from California." When they jeer and boo him, Jeff just shrugs and says, "All I can do is try to earn their respect by being who I am and doing what I do."

Jeff had saved fuel and slipped to 10th place with 21 laps to go when he decided to make his move. He threaded his way between cars and moved to fifth with 15 laps left. Two laps later, he was running third. Then Jeff made the most daring move ever seen at Daytona.

First, he slipped past Dale Earnhardt into second place. Then he pulled alongside leader Rusty Wallace. Just then Mike Skinner came up on the other side of Wallace. Together they flew down the track, three cars in a row, with Jeff low on the left.

Around Turns 1 and 2 and down the backstretch they went. Wallace pushed Jeff even lower on the track until Jeff was nearly on the apron. Up ahead Ricky Rudd's car was running slowly on the apron. Jeff was forced lower still and onto the apron, too. He came up fast behind Rudd. There was nowhere for Rudd to go. It looked as if Jeff was going to ram him from behind. At the last split-second, Jeff swerved to his right, nosed ahead of Wallace, and narrowly missed Rudd.

Suddenly Jeff was in the lead. Earnhardt moved up behind Jeff and got in his draft. They went bumper to nose for the final 10 laps. Earnhardt repeatedly tried to pass, but Jeff wiggled side to side to block him. Jeff whizzed past the checkered flag for the victory.

"I felt about the loneliest out there today that I've ever felt," Jeff said afterward. "They made sure I was left out there by myself. But you know what? I don't expect any different. And with Dale right behind me, I had a mirror-full [of company]."

Jeff's crew chief gave all the credit to his young driver. "We didn't give him the fastest car and our pit service wasn't what it should be, but we found a way," Evernham said. "In the last 10 or 12 laps, with the race on the line, it was all Jeff Gordon. It was more driver than car. He got up on that wheel and drove his heart out."

Jeff was groomed for success in racing at an early age.

2

Built for Speed

Jeff has been racing vehicles ever since he can remember. He was born August 4, 1971, in Vallejo, California, which sits atop the San Francisco Bay. Jeff was the second child born to Carol and Will Gordon. When Jeff was three months old, Carol and Will got divorced.

Jeff and his sister, Kim, who was three years old, lived with their mother. Carol supported her family by working in an office. When Jeff was a year old, his mother met a man named John Bickford. John had grown up around racetracks and he worked in the auto parts business. John's first date with Carol was an auto race at Vallejo Speedway on Labor Day

1972. Three years later they were married. Jeff called his new stepfather "Dad."

Most boys in Jeff's neighborhood were older than he was. They rode BMX bikes on a track at the end of Jeff's street. Jeff had a BMX bike, too, but it had training wheels. One day, his father suddenly removed them.

"Jeff, I've got to go to the office," his dad told him. "I'll be back in a couple of hours. You need to learn how to ride this bike or I've got to put it in the back of the truck and take it to the dump. I'm embarrassed to have it in the house if you're not going to ride it." Jeff was terrified to lose his bike. He practiced without the training wheels and learned to stay upright before his father returned home.

Jeff wanted to race his BMX bike on the track with the older boys, and his father was willing to let him. But Jeff's mother disagreed.

"I told John this is not what I wanted to see my son do," said Carol. "At BMX races, they were hauling kids away in ambulances all the time."

So what did Jeff's dad do? He bought Jeff a race car!

Jeff's mom was shocked at first. But she said, "It didn't take me long to realize that it was a lot safer than the bikes."

Jeff's race car was a **Quarter Midget,** about 6 feet long, with a small 1-cylinder, 3-horsepower engine. It was black with Jeff's nickname, "Gordy," painted on the hood. The fastest speed it could go was 20 miles per hour. Kim also got a race car. Hers was pink. She didn't like it too much.

Jeff's mom thought that racing BMX bikes would be too dangerous for her four-year-old son.

Jeff and his father cleared the weeds from a nearby field and turned it into a dirt track. Jeff practiced driving his car there.

"Once I realized, 'Hey, I can control this car,' I was fascinated by it," said Jeff. Jeff's father bought him an official racing uniform, but he insisted that four-year-old Jeff put on the uniform by himself, without help. That was how the pro racers did it, Jeff's father said, so that is how Jeff had to do it. Jeff didn't seem to mind.

Jeff got his first taste of racing when his stepfather brought home a Quarter Midget car like this one.

"We'd take that car out every night after I got home from work and run it lap after lap," said John Bickford. "Jeff couldn't seem to get enough of it."

By age five, Jeff was racing his Quarter Midget at local tracks. A year later, he began practicing in go-karts with 10-horsepower engines. At age seven, he started playing video games with an Atari system.

"*Star Wars* was really big when I was a kid," Jeff said. "I was always Luke Skywalker. The Force was with me." Though he didn't realize it at the time, playing video games helped Jeff develop quick reflexes that would be useful on the racetrack.

Jeff was small for his age. By the time he got to third grade, other kids at school would tease him. Jeff feared the bullies, but he never let them know that. A few times, he even got into fights. Before long, the bullying stopped.

Jeff was eight years old in 1979 when he became the Quarter Midget national champion. He had made a name for himself in Bay Area racing circles. His father ordered 12 dozen "Jeff Gordon" T-shirts to sell to fans. He hung the shirts in the back of the truck. As Jeff remembers, "somebody would come up, give us $12, and I'd go back and grab a shirt and give it to them."

A year later, Jeff started competing in 10-horse-power go-karts against drivers who were twice his age. Parents who were jealous of Jeff's success claimed that Jeff and his parents were lying about his age.

"We were running against guys 17 and older—unlimited age," said John Bickford. "We were still winning. And those guys were going, 'There's no darn nine-year-old kid gonna run with us! Get outta here!'"

At age 10, Jeff entered 25 local races against teenagers, and he won every race. That year he also won the Quarter Midget national title again. "My father was building a future star," said Jeff. "I was just having fun."

Jeff listened to his teachers and got good grades in school, but he was more interested in his racing. Jeff and his father often loaded Jeff's racing car on the back of the truck and traveled to tracks all over California. They couldn't afford to stay in motels, so they slept in the truck. Sometimes Jeff's mother and sister went along.

At home, John Bickford insisted that Jeff behave like a race car driver. "I used to tell Jeff if you get up in the morning and you waddle on into the kitchen and you quack when you go out there, and somebody provides you with something when you quack and you kind of conduct yourself as a duck, people will perceive you as a duck," said Bickford. "But if you get up every morning and conduct yourself like a race car driver, you dress and act like one, maybe someday in your career you'll be perceived as a race car driver. One thing's for sure, if you act like a duck, nobody's going to think you're a race car driver."

At times, the traveling and racing and acting like a race car driver got to be too much for Jeff. But the thrill of racing and winning and the desire to please his father always lured Jeff back to the track.

"He burned out on me a couple of times," said John Bickford. "He was 10 years old and he wanted to do other things. I took Jeff's whole childhood away from him."

By the age of 12, Jeff began racing a half-ton **sprint car** with a 600-horsepower engine. He and his father built their own car with parts they scrounged. But California and most other states had an age requirement for sprint car racing, and Jeff was often turned away at the track. He grew the best mustache he could with the few whiskers he had, and he drew eyebrow pencil over the whiskers to make the mustache look thicker.

Jeff managed to sneak into enough races to get a good feel for sprint racing. The following year, he went out on the national sprint car circuit. The racers there were twice his age. At first he struggled and nearly quit racing altogether. For one big race, he and his father drove 68 hours from Northern California to Florida, only to have him crash on a wet track on the first lap.

"I just can't do this, Dad," Jeff said, sobbing. He wanted to go home, but his father would not let him quit. "No," John Bickford said, "we're going to stick this thing out."

At the next race a few days later, Jeff kept up with the country's best sprint racers. His father stood watching, realizing that his son could compete with these drivers after all. "I remember thinking, 'If I don't quit him, if I stick with the program, I think we're going to have us a race car driver,'" said his father. "And that's probably the first time emotion went through my body."

Jeff and his father got tired of trying to sneak into races. During their travels they had learned that many of the racetracks in the Midwest had no age restriction. So when Jeff was 13, he moved with his family to Pittsboro, Indiana, to have better racing opportunities. Jeff practiced at a track in nearby Haubstadt. He dreamed of racing someday at another nearby track: the famed Indianapolis Motor Speedway.

Within a year, Jeff won his first sprint car race. It was at K-C Raceway in Chillicothe, Ohio. When Jeff crossed the finish line, he started bawling. His father ran down the hill to the center of the track and lifted Jeff high in the air. Then together, they both cried.

Sixteen-year-old Jeff with his winged sprint car

Jeff raced midget cars as well as sprints. He won a national championship in midget racing in 1990.

Jeff began winning regularly, but he needed a sponsor to improve his racing. He went to the Valvoline Oil Company to ask the company to sponsor him and give him free motor oil. An executive there asked Jeff how he had gotten to the office.

"My mother drove me," Jeff told him.

"Now let me get this straight," the executive said. "You drive a 650-horsepower sprint car on half-mile tracks and you had to get your mom to drive you down here?"

"Yes sir. I'm not old enough to have a driver's license."

Jeff attended Tri-West High School in Lizton. His favorite subject was science because the teacher was a racing fan who taught Jeff more about how an engine works.

Jeff competed most nights and on weekends. He often missed school on Fridays because of races. When he returned to school Monday morning, his teachers would ask him how that weekend's race had gone. Jeff would just shrug and smile. Usually, he had won but didn't want to brag about it.

Jeff in his senior year of high school

Jeff felt silly when he had to take a driver's education course in order to get his license. By then, he had already won more than 100 races.

"I probably didn't teach him a lot as far as driver's ed was concerned," said teacher Larry Sparks. Jeff got his regular driver's license the same day he got his racing license from the United States Automobile Club (USAC).

Jeff was voted prom king in high school.

Jeff and his best friend, Todd Osborne, played pool, rode skateboards, and played video games. They ran together on the cross-country team, built engines for their race cars, and beat older kids at local races.

Racing helped make Jeff popular at school, and his classmates voted him the king of his senior prom. He even entered a race on the night of his high school graduation.

"Most of my time was spent racing, so I did miss out on some of the things the other kids did," Jeff said of his childhood. "But I have never regretted it."

Jeff drove a white Ford sponsored by Baby Ruth on the Busch Grand National circuit.

Into the Big Time

"This is it!" Jeff screamed into the telephone. "This is what I want to do for the rest of my life!"

Jeff had called his mother from NASCAR legend Buddy Baker's driving school in North Carolina. Jeff had just driven his first stock car. He loved the great power of the car and the way it hugged the track.

"I knew right away that stock car racing was the way I wanted to go," Jeff later recalled. "The car wasn't like anything I was used to. I loved it."

Jeff and his father found a sponsor named Bill Davis who agreed to pay for Jeff's car in return for a percentage of Jeff's winnings. Jeff promptly joined NASCAR's Busch Grand National circuit, which is one step lower than the top-level Winston Cup circuit. At age 18, Jeff was the youngest driver on the circuit. "I'm ready to rub fenders with anyone," he said confidently.

Jeff still competed in other forms of racing. He won the 1990 USAC Midget Championship and the 1991 AMA Grand National Dirt Track Series championship. But it was on the Grand National circuit that he emerged as a daredevil racer.

After a few decent performances, he realized the value of a talented pit crew. He asked a friend named Andy Petri for help.

"I was in New Jersey when Andy Petri called," said Ray Evernham, a former racer who had become a pit crew chief. Evernham went to meet Jeff. Evernham says Jeff looked like a 14-year-old when he first saw him. When Jeff opened his briefcase, the older man saw a cell phone and a Nintendo game. Evernham recalls wondering *Just who was this kid?* But he reluctantly agreed to work with Jeff. They were partners until the fall of 1999 when Evernham left to form a new team for the Daimler-Chrysler corporation.

In 1992, Jeff won a record 11 poles. The pole is the inside front row position at the start of a race. It goes to the fastest racer in the single-car qualifying runs that are generally held the day before the race. Jeff turned his good starting positions into three Grand National victories, winning twice in Charlotte, North Carolina, and once in Atlanta, Georgia.

Jeff's first win at Atlanta Motor Speedway came against the best pro stock car racers in the world. Top-level Winston Cup racers sometimes compete in lower-level Grand National events to check out the track. Jeff drove fast and loose with his back tires skidding from side to side as he struggled to keep up with the veterans.

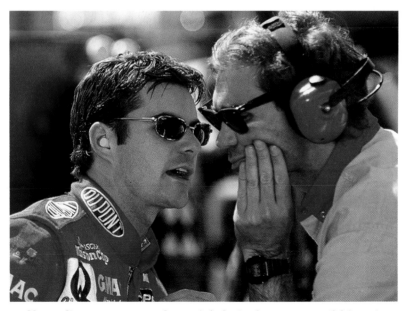

Jeff credits Ray Evernham (right) for many of his wins.

Rick Hendrick spotted Jeff on the Busch Grand National circuit and signed him to the Hendrick Motorsports team.

One man watching from the stands could hardly believe his eyes. Rick Hendrick, a multimillionaire car dealer who managed two Winston Cup drivers, watched Jeff's white car push right up behind the leaders Harry Gant and Dale Earnhardt. Hendrick said to a friend, "Man, that guy's gonna wreck. No one can drive a car that loose for long." But Jeff kept his car on the track, and he out-maneuvered Gant and Earnhardt and the rest of the field to capture the checkered flag.

Hendrick sat stunned. He asked who the winning driver was. Someone told him that it was "that kid, Gordon." When Hendrick learned that Bill Davis had not re-signed Jeff to a new contract for the coming season, he offered to sponsor the kid. Jeff did not hesitate to say yes.

Hendrick Motorsports is an elaborate complex of buildings near Charlotte, North Carolina. The shop for Jeff's car was 10,000 square feet, about the size of a small building, with 15 crew members. Rick Hendrick's other two drivers—Terry Labonte and Ken Schrader—welcomed Jeff to the team. Jeff would drive car number 24, a Chevy painted red, blue, green, and yellow. Jeff would wear a matching uniform, and his team would eventually be called the Rainbow Warriors.

Jeff moved with his parents to Charlotte. He joined the Winston Cup circuit in time for the 1992 season finale, which was held at the track where Hendrick had discovered the young driver—Atlanta Motor Speedway. The 1992 race was Jeff's first against the top drivers. Bill Elliott barely beat Alan Kulwicki, the Winston Cup champion of that year, to win the race.

The race was the last for famous driver Richard Petty, known as "The King." Petty's car was in a fiery crash on lap 95 of the race. The legendary racer finished 35th and announced his retirement not long after the race. Representing the next generation of greats, Jeff finished 31st in the 42-car race. He couldn't wait for the 1993 season.

Jeff broke onto the Winston Cup circuit in 1993.

Here Comes "The Kid"

Jeff opened his rookie season at Daytona International Speedway with a record-breaking win. At age 21, he became the youngest driver ever to win a 125-mile qualifying race. He was also the first rookie to do it since the famed Johnny Rutherford had 30 years earlier.

"It's unbelievable," Jeff said. "If you were on my radio scanner, you would have heard a whole lot of screaming excitement." In the big 500-mile race the next day, Jeff was in second place with two laps to go and finished fifth.

But Jeff's favorite part of the weekend at Daytona did not even occur on the asphalt track. Each year, a young woman is selected as "Miss Winston," and she represents the NASCAR circuit that year. Her job is to promote the sport and present the trophy to each winner in victory lane. The 1993 Miss Winston was Brooke Sealey, a student at the University of North Carolina.

Jeff had seen a picture of Brooke. He had called her several times for a date, but Brooke did not return Jeff's calls. NASCAR had a rule that Miss Winstons could not date drivers. "I was wowed before I ever met her," Jeff said.

On the morning of Jeff's qualifying race, he finally met Brooke. It was Valentine's Day, and Brooke gave him some little heart-shaped candies for good luck. Then Jeff won the race.

Jeff's wife, Brooke

In victory lane, Brooke handed Jeff the winner's trophy and gave him the customary kiss on the cheek. Afterward, they talked. "He was so sweet," Brooke said, "and so down to earth."

Jeff and Brooke decided to start dating in spite of the rule. They went on secret dates to movies and restaurants. If other drivers suddenly appeared, Brooke slipped out a side entrance. One night at a restaurant, Brooke asked Jeff if he had ever considered shaving off his mustache. Jeff left the table for a few minutes and returned with his mustache gone.

Out on the racetrack, Jeff was making mistakes and learning. At North Wilkesboro Speedway, he was running loose when his back tires skidded out and sent him careening into a wall. His car burst into flames. Quickly he pressed two buttons, one that shuts off the car's electricity and the other that activates a fire extinguisher that sprays in the cockpit. He climbed out of the car unhurt.

At Atlanta Motor Speedway, Jeff was in the lead with 12 laps to go when he pitted for a splash of fuel. The stop took just a few seconds, but he returned to the track in fourth place, and Morgan Shepherd won instead. Jeff's crew, the Rainbow Warriors, changed strategy at Michigan International Speedway. They reduced the car's horsepower slightly to save fuel. When the other cars pitted late in the race for fuel, Jeff kept right on going to take second place.

Jeff finished second again at Charlotte Motor Speedway, prompting crew chief Ray Evernham to say, "I don't think anybody knows just how talented Jeff Gordon is. Even Jeff doesn't know." Other racers were beginning to find out. Midway through the season, Jeff was in 10th place in the Cup points standings. Veteran Dale Earnhardt said, "He's the best young talent that's ever been out here."

Jeff finished the year 14th overall and was an easy choice for Rookie of the Year. "We had a good year," he said. "I learned a lot and I had the opportunity to race with the best drivers in the world." But Jeff yearned for more.

A new Miss Winston was named for the 1994 season, and Brooke's duties were over. At a restaurant the night before the first race of the season at Daytona, Jeff proposed marriage. Brooke said yes. The couple then announced their engagement to stunned NASCAR drivers. They got married later that year. Ray Evernham was Jeff's best man. The reception featured a seven-foot high wedding cake. Afterward, Jeff and Brooke moved to a large home on Lake Norman near Charlotte where other race car drivers live.

Jeff did not have to travel far from home for the Coca-Cola 600 at Charlotte. In that race, the 11th of the season, Jeff was locked in a duel with Rusty Wallace and Geoff Bodine with 20 laps to go. All three drivers pitted for fuel and fresh tires. Wallace and Bodine got all four tires replaced, but Jeff's crew changed only his two right-side tires, which saved a few seconds in the pit. Jeff returned to the track in the lead and never surrendered it. The victory was his first NASCAR points race win.

"With about 10 laps to go, I had such a good feeling," said Jeff. "We pretty much held the gap on Rusty, and I started crying out there in the race car. You can't imagine how hard it is to get to this point. It's just wonderful, it just truly is."

Miss Winston handed the trophy to Jeff in victory lane and he cried again. Other drivers cringed at the sight of Jeff in tears. Race car drivers were supposed to be tough, they said, not emotional. They ridiculed Jeff, but he did not apologize. "I'm not ashamed to say I bawled my eyes out," he said. "This is the greatest moment of my life, a memory and feeling I'll never forget."

Jeff doesn't try to hide his emotions after a win.

Six weeks later, Jeff scored an even greater victory when he won the inaugural Brickyard 400 at Indianapolis Motor Speedway. With his friends and family among the more than 100,000 people looking down from the stands, Jeff battled Ernie "Swervin" Irvan around the track and wore him down the last few laps to take the checkered flag.

Jeff was so emotional as he took his victory lap that he had to go around the track a second time to calm down. Even members from other pit crews were happy for Jeff as they hung over the pit wall and flashed the victory sign.

"I just can't control my emotions at a time like this," said Jeff. "But I don't want to be known as a crybaby all the time. I wanted to wipe away the tears, so that's why I took the extra lap."

Jeff and Brooke celebrated the victory by eating a pineapple pizza while watching a replay of the race on the TV in their hotel room. Jeff didn't even know he had won $613,000 until he read the newspaper the next day. That's when he also saw that he had been given a new nickname: "The Kid."

At the 1994 Brickyard 400, Jeff won the first major stock car race at the Indianapolis Motor Speedway.

Jeff with his car at the Daytona 500 in 1995

5

Way Ahead

Jeff roared out front in 1995 and never looked back. He won the season's second race at Rockingham speedway in Charlotte, won again two weeks later at Atlanta Motor Speedway, and won two weeks after that in Bristol, Tennessee. He built such a commanding lead in the points race that other drivers groused that they were left racing for second place.

Jeff didn't talk about his chance of winning the Cup, but his father said, "I get so proud of him that I think my shirt buttons will flip off. I wish every parent out there could enjoy the pride that I have in Jeff."

During a five-month stretch through summer and

into fall, Jeff showed his consistency by finishing in the top 10 in 14 straight races. "Jeff is the smartest driver I've ever met, for two reasons," said Ray Evernham. "First, he has a better handle on car control than anyone I've ever seen. And second, when the car isn't 100 percent, he doesn't prescribe the cure to me, he just gives me the symptoms and lets me figure out the cure."

Jeff waits in his car during practice for the 1995 NAPA 500 at Atlanta Motor Speedway. He would go on that year to win his first points title.

Jeff cruised to the Cup series title to become, at age 24, the youngest champion in the modern era. "It's just too good to be true," he said. Some drivers complained that Jeff was too clean-cut to represent NASCAR as a champion. "He'll probably have them serve milk instead of champagne at the banquet," said one. Such comments made Jeff laugh. At the annual postseason party in New York, Jeff sat on-stage, poured himself a glass of milk, winked at the drivers, and toasted the crowd.

Jeff became an overnight sensation. Suddenly there were Jeff Gordon souvenirs of all sorts. Besides the usual clothing items like T-shirts, caps, and jackets, there were Jeff Gordon sunglasses, earrings, key chains, coffee mugs, lamps, seat cushions, beach towels, and yo-yos. Companies bombarded Jeff with pleas to endorse their products and appear in their ad campaigns. The media crush was so overwhelming that Jeff hired a team to handle his requests, including an agent, business manager, and public relations manager. "I look at it as part of my job, and I just do the best job I can," he said. "I need to work hard on and off the racetrack. But the demands are all pretty unbelievable."

Jeff hadn't lived in Indiana for several years, but

Pittsboro residents proudly erected a sign at the city limits that read:

Pittsboro Welcomes You
The Home of Jeff Gordon
NASCAR Driver

Jeff was such a celebrity at his hometown of Lake Norman that fans regularly gathered outside his house in hopes of seeing him. He and Brooke even spotted fans videotaping the family cat. Jeff appeared on TV talk shows and even got to fly in an acrobatic jet with the Blue Angels. (But when the jet flew upside down, Jeff threw up.) His fame didn't always mean Jeff got special treatment, however.

Jeff was speeding one day on his way to the airport. A police officer pulled up behind him and motioned him to pull over. "I'm Jeff Gordon," he said to the police officer. "Do you follow racing?" The police officer just kept writing the ticket. "Yeah," replied the officer. "I'm a Dale Earnhardt fan. Here's your ticket."

Jeff won at Richmond, Darlington, Bristol, Talladega . . . and on and on in 1996. He won 10 of the circuit's 33 races, proving he was the most dominant driver in NASCAR. He earned $3.5 million. He also earned the respect of his fellow drivers. As veteran driver Dale Jarrett said, "It should be illegal to be that young, that good-looking, and that talented."

Some fans claimed Jeff hadn't worked hard enough to earn his success. Even legends Darrell Waltrip and Richard Petty struggled early. The great Cale Yarborough won just once in his first nine years of racing. Jeff made winning look like a breeze. Some fans wore T-shirts that showed Jeff's rainbow-colored car smashed and upside down with the words, "The Way It Ought To Be." They formed an Anti-Gordon Fan Club. Other athletes came to Jeff's defense.

Whatever people said about him, Jeff kept winning.

"Where does it say you have to get beat up and knocked around before people think you've paid your dues?" asked Darrell Waltrip. "If you're good, you're good. Why should it matter how or when you got here? Jeff doesn't deserve this."

Basketball star Charles Barkley said, "When I was growing up, everyone hated the Boston Celtics because they always won. Jeff Gordon is going through the same thing. When you think about it, there is no way possible that any person in the entire world should dislike him. What has he ever done except win?"

Kyle Petty, himself a rising race star, pointed out that Jeff's success helped other auto racers. "When Jeff goes on the Letterman TV show," said Petty, "he takes all of us with him. His success has been great for NASCAR and every one of us."

Jeff ignored all the fuss. He concentrated on other things, such as his charitable work with the Leukemia Society. Leukemia is a kind of cancer, often striking children, that causes an abnormal increase of white blood cells in the tissues and often in the blood. Ray Evernham's son, Ray Jr., was suffering from leukemia, and Jeff gave hundreds of thousands of dollars to help find a cure. Then, before the start of the 1997 season, Jeff heard some terrible news. Car owner Rick Hendrick had leukemia, too.

At the opener at Daytona, Hendrick's three drivers raced their hearts out for their ailing owner. They finished one-two-three with Jeff the winner. The following week, Jeff won again. As Hendrick watched each race from his home in North Carolina, Jeff racked up 10 victories to win the points title again. "I got you that gold car trophy!" he told Hendrick at season's end. This time, Jeff had won a record $6 million in prize money.

Jeff, Terry Labonte (left), and Ricky Craven (right) honored Rick Hendrick with their victories at Daytona.

In 1997 Jeff won his second Winston Cup points title.

A race car driver needs quick reflexes, and Jeff works on his quickness by playing video games. His favorite games are Madden Football, Triple Play Baseball, and NASCAR '98. He even coproduced his own racing video game.

"Don't ever challenge him at video games," says Jeff's manager. "You'll lose. He's very, very good."

Jeff used his blinding quickness in 1998 like never before. How could he possibly top two 10-win seasons in a row? By winning 13 times! The total matched Richard Petty's modern-era record. Jeff captured the points title again while earning more than $9 million for the Rainbow Warriors.

The Rainbow Warriors

*Brooke congratulates Jeff for winning the 1999
Daytona 500.*

Jeff's favorite victory came at the Indianapolis Motor Speedway when he held off a furious charge by Mark Martin as thousands of hometown supporters cheered Jeff on. "I usually don't hear a roar like that," Jeff said. "When the race was over and I came down pit road, I actually shut off the engine. I had to hear it. It was awesome to hear that many people cheer."

Jeff gave auto racing a big boost when he was selected as one of five finalists for the ESPY Man of the Year award. Superstar sports achievers Tiger Woods, Terrell Davis, Sammy Sosa, and Mark McGwire were the other finalists.

"It's an honor just to be included with such sports heroes," Jeff said. "I have great parents who gave me the opportunity to be a race car driver. To see the way it's all worked out, it makes my parents heroes in my mind."

No one was surprised to see Jeff open the 1999 season with a victory at Daytona. He won more than $2 million for that race alone. He followed with five more victories, including two with new crew chief Brian Whitesell.

With all his winnings, Jeff and Brooke can live a fantasy life. They own two mansions, a 45-foot motor home, a 29-foot speedboat, and a Lear jet. Jeff also gives a lot of money away. He donates generously to the Make-A-Wish Foundation and cancer research. He created an organization called Kids and the Hood that supports children's causes. He teams with PBS television to teach viewers about the math and science used in racing. "As racing becomes more and more of a mainstream sport," says Jeff, "the opportunity to use its popularity to teach kids increases." Jeff has a simple message: "Don't Ever Quit."

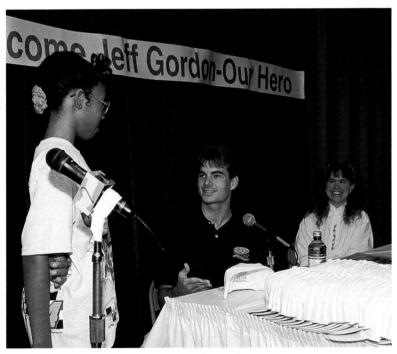

Jeff fields questions at a Kids and the Hood event.

Jeff has shattered so many racing records that it's easy to forget how young he is. At the start of the twenty-first century he was still just 28 years old.

"I have to admit, at my age, you're not expected to do all this," says Jeff. "This has turned into so much more than I ever anticipated. It's amazing to me I've gotten this far."

"How far can Jeff go?" says former crew chief Evernham. "As far as he wants. There is no limit."

Career Highlights

Statistics

Year	Races	Wins	Top 5	Top 10	Poles	Earnings	Point Standings
1992	1	0	0	0	0	$6,285	x
1993	30	0	7	11	1	$765,168	14th
1994	31	2	7	14	1	$1,779,523	8th
1995	31	7	17	23	8	$4,347,343	1st
1996	31	10	21	24	5	$3,428,485	2nd
1997	32	10	22	23	1	$6,375,658	1st
1998	33	13	26	28	7	$9,306,584	1st
1999	35	7	19	22	7	$5,281,361	6th
Career	224	49	119	145	30	$31,290,407	

Honors

- Won Quarter Midget national championship in 1979 and 1981
- Won USAC Midget Championship in 1990
- Won National Dirt Track Championship in 1991
- Named NASCAR Rookie of the Year in 1993
- Won Winston Cup points title in 1995
- Won Winston Cup points title in 1997
- Named True Value Man of the Year in 1997
- Won Winston Cup points title in 1998
- Named ESPY Man of the Year finalist in 1998

Glossary

apron: The paved area between the racetrack surface and the infield grass.

backstretch: The back straightaway on an oval, opposite the starting line.

horsepower: The power a horse produces in pulling. A horse can pull 330 pounds a distance of 100 feet in one minute.

pit stop: A pause in the race when the driver pulls into a designated spot and his or her car is adjusted and fueled.

Quarter Midget: A race car that is larger than a go-kart but smaller than a sprint car. It has an open cockpit and reaches speeds of up to 115 miles an hour.

sprint car: A race car that is larger than a Quarter Midget but smaller than a stock car. It has a powerful engine and a tall, narrow shape.

Sources

Information for this book was obtained from the following sources: Jerry Adler (*Newsweek*, 28 July 1997); Tom Cotter (*Road & Track*, February 1999); Ed Hinton (*Sports Illustrated*, 22 February 1999); Lucy Howard (*Newsweek*, 1 March 1999); Jonathan Ingram (*On Track*, 3 June 1999); Tom Jensen (*Winston Cup Illustrated*, April 1999); Claire B. Lang (*Winston Cup Illustrated*, March 1999); Steve Lopez (*Time*, 31 May 1999); Bill Lovell (*Sport*, March 1999); Bill McGuire (*AutoWeek*, 21 June 1999); Chris O'Malley (*Popular Science*, April 1999); Al Pearce (*Auto Week*, 22 February 1999); Erik Spanberg (*Business Journal Serving Charlotte & the Metropolitan Area*, 28 December 1998); Peter Spiegel (*Forbes*, 14 December 1998); Staff (*Sports Illustrated*, 28 December 1998); Staff (*Sports Illustrated for Kids*, July 1999); Staff (*Time for Kids*, 26 February 1999); Gary L. Thomas (*Jeff Gordon.* Los Angeles: Renaissance Books, 1999); Stephen Thompson (*Brandweek*, 12 July 1999); Alex Tresniowski (*People*, 30 June 1997); Steve Waid (*Winston Cup Illustrated*, October 1998).

Index

Write to Jeff:

You can send mail to Jeff at the address on the right. If you write a letter, don't get your hopes up too high. Jeff and other athletes get lots of letters every day, and they aren't always able to answer them all. You can visit Jeff Gordon's Official Home Page at www.jeffgordon.com.

Jeff Gordon
Performance PR Plus
529 North College Street
Charlotte, NC 28202

Acknowledgments

Photographs reproduced with permission of: © SportsChrome East/West, pp. 1, 2, 11, 44, 54; © ALLSPORT USA/Craig Jones, pp. 3, 15, 59; © SportsChrome East/West/Greg Crisp, pp. 6, 13, 14, 32, 38, 40, 55; © ALLSPORT USA/David Taylor, pp. 9, 18, 35; © Vince Streano/Corbis, p. 21; © Stephanie Maze/Corbis, p. 22; © John Mahoney, pp. 27, 28; © Seth Poppel Yearbook Archives, pp. 29, 30; © AP/Wide World Photos, pp. 36, 48; © James Cutler, pp. 45, 46; © ALLSPORT USA/Robert LaBerge, p. 51; © ALLSPORT USA/Andy Lyons, p. 53; © ALLSPORT USA/Jamie Squire, p. 56; © Tom Raymond, courtesy Dupont Company, p. 58.

Front cover photographs by © ALLSPORT USA/Craig Jones (right); © ALLSPORT USA/David Taylor (left); © ALLSPORT/USA Andy Lyons (background). Back cover photograph by © Tom Raymond, courtesy Dupont Company.

Artwork by Michael Tacheny.

About the Author

Jeff Savage is the author of more than 80 sports books for young readers, including LernerSports biographies of Julie Foudy, Sammy Sosa, and Mark McGwire.